Lock Him Up!

Lock Him Up!

Looking beyond the Person Trump

CHARLES DEWINTER MSc, MBA

ISBN-13: 9781974425792
ISBN-10: 1974425797

For Carla

On Content

This is a Post-Truth, Trump-current, pre-madness book.

It doesn't contain facts, statistics, or any other data.

Nothing needs to be true or even plausible.

Here is a book of fiction despite the analogies with the real world.

It simply aims at entertaining your dulled mind and your scared-stiff guts better than the media and the daily news do.

This book is written as a stream of consciousness.

Half of it is intuition, not checked for logic.

The second half is based on pattern recognition of history by shooting from the hip.

And the third half is based on a deep feeling that something is really rotten in this world and on this planet.

It is narrated as a saddening farce for your entertainment only.

On Style

I will be direct and ruthless, and, depending on my inspiration, I hope to be vulgar at times.

It is of course difficult to forget one's good education in writing a book like this, but I shall certainly try.

Forgive me if any decency is left in the text. I am trying hard to be a child of my times.

Vulgarity seems to be considered these days a necessary survival skill. It can be learned quite fast, and in this way, it seemingly stands in opposition to learning to be elegant and noble, which take a lifetime to accomplish.

And if you believed you had finally acquired this savoir faire—like some nouveaux riches do—it just means that you are not even halfway.

World, June 2017

One

SETTING THE SCENE

Everyone asks *which turn* the United States eventually will take under the presidency of Donald Trump. And *how fast?*

This book aims at peering right through the talk and capers of President Trump and his entourage.

The future is like a puzzle, of which we only see the present pieces of uncertainty. These manifest themselves less by what is said than by what is being decided and done.

The acuity resides in piecing them together, until a picture emerges "that makes sense"—that is, one that exemplifies the consistency, common sense, and psychological insight of human beings.

This drawing then becomes one of the possible realities of tomorrow that shall unfold out of today's moment and out of the policy decisions of the present men in power.

In the specific case of this book, we shall, on the basis of partial information and in the absence of a formal announcement to the citizens of the United States in which direction the White House will take the country, try to reconstruct a "total picture" of the "new all-encompassing world order."

All the same.

This probably becomes a guide for our insight into "the plan for change," which a few folks have cooked up and under the leadership of President Trump (? or Pence) shall be turned into concrete policies and decisions by the White House and the current administration.

The leaders of the United States and their decisions will have serious implications, domestically as well as abroad.

> Never doubt that a small group of thoughtful, committed citizens can change the world. Indeed, it's the only thing that ever has. (Margaret Mead)

But committed to what?

In this piece of writing, I mainly try—with malicious pleasure as well as respect for the president—to ignore Trump's declarations and tweets in my thinking.

But what is behind the…

"Words, words, words!"

His executive orders, memorandums, and so on are much more interesting than his tweets.

This booklet does not depart from a fascination for Trump as a character, about whom everyone each day wants to know whether Donnie had a good meal and on whose head he has shit this time.

This hunger for sensation is of course the media's bread and butter, and granted, he does not let them starve.

This book instead tries to see through what is said, to what people in and behind power do, and what their mental background is.

We have to understand all of this to understand their wishes, ambitions, and future decisions.

I derive my inspiration in the jostle of "spoken" opinions from what one sees happening: facts, which are susceptible to different interpretations anyway, but certainly "food for forward thinking."

- Which person(s) has (have) placed Trump (and his confidantes) in which places?
- What are their backgrounds and their risk-taking profiles?
- Can we understand—less *what* but—*why* he says what he says, and what plausible interpretations of this in a personal and also wider (inter)national context are?
- Why is he unpredictable? And might this serve a purpose?
- Which groups do benefit from his executive orders as opposed to those about who he *says* he will "surprise big…"
- Who, in his own words, does he despise, and who will he crush? What does he really do? Whom does he offer a brighter future by his decisions, not his threats?
- How strong are the groups he frequently despised during his campaign and to this day? Are they well organized?

- In short, are these scapegoat groups financially influential in New York or politically well connected in Washington or both? Are they an influential factor in his policy making? Reelection? Or can his executive administration just roll over them under the guise of Trump legislative decisional power?

This book aims to lay the strategic puzzle for a possible but—so far—unknown "new world order." The pieces of the puzzle are known in the mind of master strategists involved, but for us—the populace—today only a few pieces lie face up and visible on the table. Every piece is a fact or a decision.

"No palabras—no tweetos!"

Most pieces of the puzzle—that is to say, those decisions that await announcement and will shed light on the future way forward—still lie face down, until Trump and his direct advisers and possibly the top of his administration shall turn them over one after one, by way of their decisions over time.

The guesswork about the future decisions of Trump and company written on the bottom of the pieces of the puzzle that have been turned up and will reveal how exactly the total picture of the puzzle—or the American view on the new world order—actually looks is called strategic thinking.

Like in so many TV quizzes, making guesses about the total picture implies more chance that we err.

But no sweat.

On the basis of current incomplete data, others will arrive at a totally different blueprint for the future of what the hidden design of the puzzle looks like.

Post-Truth has many veiled faces.

But one needs the nerve to conceive all possible drawings of the hidden puzzle.

For those not participating in the decision-making process and not sitting around the table at the White House—and neither are lobbyists or representatives of the respected groups who, *derrière les coulisses,* wield their heavy influence on future policies—imagining such possible alternatives is the only meaningful attempt at their disposal to understand how the Trump presidency influences their own lives and their well-being in the future, and how to give a timely response.

The solution of the strategic puzzle presented here or, in other words, the predicted "strategic new world order" of White House and company lies in the following summary:

America first! Supremacy today…supremacy forever!

To achieve this goal and sustain/enforce its economic and military supremacy, all preparations need to be taken to go to war with China.

Hence, the current world order based on friendly globalization is to be terminated. Globalization is no bad thing per se. On the contrary.

From a perspective of a nascent leadership battle, however, borders need to be closed and preparations need to be taken…

Exit globalization.

War with China

The rest of what is displayed in today's political theater, what is said, not said, quarreled about, the pleasing, the lying, and the schmoozing are side issues, smokescreens, lightning bolts, or hidden and misunderstood parts of the preparations.

This is not a book about an obscure conspiration theory.

Although speaking openly about an upcoming war is taboo, one should never ever think about geopolitics while totally dismissing the possibility of war.

Hence the attention here for this geo-alternative future.

———

The rest of this book is divided into four more chapters:

(2) Imagining a New World Order, (3) Prepare the Hearts and Minds of the American People for War, (4) Rethink the International Chessboard of Strategic Alliances, and the Epilogue.

Two

Imagining a New World Order

The one-million-dollar question

The whole time there is speculation about "the plan" of President Trump.

In all media this question came up constantly:

Does he have one or not? A plan.

And if he does have a plan, then what is it?

And if you were to neatly pile up his declarations, tweets, and intentions, really no insight emerges into what people who habitually make plans would call a plan.

At first sight Trump's sayings seem to follow the direction in which his fingers are pointed.

Whatever Donald Trump calls his "plan" bears a closer resemblance to the chaotic plan of execution of Theresa May and company since the Brexit decision than, for instance, to the masterful political-demagogic plan with which tactical genius Erdoğan wiped out the entire intellectual opposition in no time.

Let's face it; to be completely "surprised"—in Erdoğan's own words that is—by a military coup d'état and within a week to finalize a list with the names of thirty thousand people who went to prison in no time and another two hundred thousand who were fired from their jobs…now that's what you really call preparing for a plan.

Trump's neurons

Besides, is a character like Donald Trump even capable of making a plan? Can the neurons in his head be seduced to doing that? All axioms, meekly and very structurally pegged to the thread of carefully considered logic? I don't think so.

By nature, Trump is an opportunist and a dealmaker, a dazzling narcissist and a fantastic storyteller—in short, a blabbermouth!

To make plans, however, requires the skill to not think of oneself for a minute but how to attain a very precise and carefully defined goal.

Planning requires a mind game of tennis with time as your adversary.

But to do this, Donnie is too impulsive, too narcissistic, too vain. Making mega, big, risky, difficult plans that require pain, hardship, and misery is a skill of the stubborn, tenacious, straight-lined, cold-blooded, and sometimes cruel leaders.

Mike Pence seems to come close.

Donnie, on the other hand, seems just like a doll to me to go on holiday with. No preparation necessary.

Cool and easy.

We start driving and see where we arrive, and on the road, we have as much fun as we can. Anything goes, and anything is possible, because we have the charming mug, the masterly street talk, and the cash in our pockets.

So given his personality and the fact that absolutely nothing about a plan has surfaced so far, not even a few outlines that with a lot of effort would appear on the horizon of what we can imagine, conceive, capture from his words and decisions, I conclude: Donald goes in all directions. Donald is brilliant, but…

"Donald has no plan."

Donald didn't have a "plan" and still hasn't got one…

So no plan?

Even if Donald Trump did not come up with a new world order and the suitable route plan that comes with it, by no means this is the sign for there being no plan at all.

Of course there is a plan, that is to say, in the making!

You don't go for a new world order, as is constantly said and feared in the media, without a route plan mapping out the big changes, even if you limit yourself merely to very big outlines.

You can just about shoot a country like Afghanistan to perdition without any plan that ensures that later life for the population becomes somewhat cozier or more humane than before. But if you want to drive through a new world order, there isn't much room for improvisation.

A new world order isn't created *à l'improviste* by a few wise guys who are bored and simply for the sake of wanting something new decide to cook up a new world order together and see it to fruition next.

The basis for a new world order for society is deeply embedded in the zeitgeist

A plan is something you make as soon as you can envisage a clear and straightforward *final objective* that you are at pains to reach. This is a plan's necessary condition: whoever doesn't know where he wants to go on vacation cannot book his plane tickets.

A new world order starts with a new vision on the future of the planet as a whole and on the rules of conduct that shall be in effect. And this new order has to cut its ties with the old one.

Sometimes the final objective of what a newly created world order should/could be isn't clear from the beginning. Not even for its planners.

History, economic development, and societal changes are never the product of rational processes.

They are born from the underbelly of life and society itself.

The "zeitgeist," as the Germans call it, is the pressure cooker of deep socioeconomic change in the underbelly of society. When the belly of society gets angry, things are about to happen. Big things!

Politicians do not capture this spirit of the times.
They are always late.

Politics does not have a radar system at its disposal for what lives in the underbelly of society.

It is too preoccupied for that and with maintaining its power.

It doesn't care about the populace.

It never did, except for some very brief periods in history in some countries.

And if power ever had such an early-warning system, *"Warning, warning, belly changes ahead,"* then still it would only ever use it to try constipating this underbelly until belly pains, cramps, and misery become so bad that incredible societal diarrhea ensues, a purge of cropped-up misery from which emerge very painful confrontations between the belly and the head of society.

Dead in the streets.

Torture in prisons.

Silence at home.

And then follows revolution.

- The French Revolution in 1789 against the arrogance of the French monarchy and its corruption.
- The Spring of Nations in 1848 when in several European countries street rebellions against hunger and the exploitation by big capital broke out simultaneously. Result: twelve thousand shot dead in the streets.
- The Bolshevik Revolution in October 1917 against the Russian empire.
- The Prague Spring in 1968 when the "Mighty" of the USSR wasn't quite pleased by the belly-ish laments of the masses craving new and more free liberalism in Czechoslovakia.
- The Iranian Revolution in 1979 against the Shah.
- Tiananmen Square in China in April 1989.
- The Fall of the Berlin Wall in November 1989.
- The Arab Spring (and Winter) or the independent democratic uprisings across the Arab world in 2011.

- Venezuelan uprisings in 2016.
- Erdoğan…
- Brexit…
- *Trump…*
- ?

Democracy is a lousy governance concept for running a country but quite excellent for helping the belly of society organize the rebound when power goes ballistic in greed, corruption, and neglect of its citizens.

When power starts to treat its citizens like dogs, the belly of society roars, and the populace gets angry and decides to put a stop to the pain that is inflicted to it.

And the dogs go wild.

My dear, the very rich and the powerful ones, beware of the wild dogs on your doorstep. They may become far more dangerous than the barbarians were at the gate of your companies.

If we want to understand why so many Americans agree with Trump's professed intention of a new world order, we need to understand the belly of American society.

The underbelly of American society

- The Tea Party is angry: a belly-driven move against liberal ideas and freedom of expression;
- The Alt Right is angry: a belly-driven white Caucasian reflex against the multicultural tolerant society, which feels threatened by immigrants from Latin America and the Middle East or, if you want, by all the "chocolatitos"—that is to say, all the not-so-white-of-skins;
- A lot of people hate the arrogance of the government administration that swamps the country with useless paper and regulatory shit that corrupt Washington politics poisons society with;
- The losers and detractors of the global economy are angry: a big and so far silent group, crushed by the all-dominant narrative that globalization is the world's blessing, but who have suffered tremendously from globalization (digitization and soon robotization are yet to come);
- Apocalyptic levels of inequality have finally made the losing middle class angry; American people used to look up at people who got rich. When someone got rich, he had created a lot of jobs in the process and deserved respect for his/her achievement;

- Today, the ones who get very rich are frequently job destroyers. Fat investment bankers, hedge-fund managers, private equity partners, Uber, Airbnb shareholders all get rich by sucking society and the economy dry of regular jobs. Only an idiot is incapable of seeing that the rules of the economic game have changed. That most rich got there, not with the help of the workers but at their expense.

- And perhaps something else: it may not yet be felt so strongly by the populace but definitely by the broad layer of society above. Americans looking East to Asia, especially China, are worried they cannot sustain world leadership and wealth creation in the future as has been done for the last thirty years. Concern about the rise of Eastern military and economic powers.

This is a *busy belly,* if you ask me.

Lots of bile concealed and waiting to be mobilized…

An Alka-Seltzer won't do the job this time.

And lots of testosterone in the underbelly waiting to explode…

Lots of emotions.
Lots of anger and despair.
Lots of insecurity.
Lots of fear.
Lot of "againsts."
Lots of nervousness.
Lots of negative energy.

Warning, warning: "Belly roaring!"

"Spatter diarrhea ahead!"

This synchronicity of fear, despair, and anger, if not rage, leads to a groundswell, a mind-set of heaviness in the American belly.

No wonder that our Western society becomes so obese.

The explanation is not only with the corrupt lobbyists of the food and sugar industry.

Is not our body also the psychosomatic mirror image of the lightness or heaviness of our emotional life and our level of fear or happiness in society?

Populists capture the zeitgeist

The so-called rebels who scream that the end of the societal model is near are being treated as populists by the political establishment.

They are being trashed by the media.

Populism sounds like an insult.

But the masses, hitherto silent under the yoke of what was preached as the truth in the traditional socioeconomic model, instantly hail them back—invigorated by the sudden realization that they feel and think alike with a whole bunch of other people—and put them on a pedestal under a roar of applause.

The success of populism finds its roots in the disdain of the current political and rich class that neglected the minimal well-being of the populace.

Populists themselves are often no good planners.

Instead, they have a keen sense of where the zeitgeist and the world are headed.

And they can put this in marvelous words too.

But they don't know what to do with it.

The "doing" is what strategic planners organize.

But you don't often find those on the street.

They are neatly hidden in the offices of influential groups, whose interests they defend and for whom change is only an opportunity to sustain their power and wealth.

Strategists have a good nose for identifying those who have the gift of intuition and who can phrase wonderfully: *the populists!*—the fashion designers of society.

Behind every star populist, at least one interest group is hiding, which, under the guise of "help," hijacks his thoughts, his popularity and for which this populist is merely a puppet of their own interests…

He will manage the crowds. They will manage him.

Farsighted strategists and also first and foremost businesspeople regard it as their first interest to timely pick up these signals from the underbelly of society (to divert them, to exploit them).

Politicians feel these symptoms too, but they're in complete denial, because after all they helped create what society inherits today—for example, globalization.

Strategists do wonder: Who are today's rainmakers for change? Who has his intuitive antennae so finely tuned to or deeply rooted in society's discontent?

Who is this psycho-belly doctor?

That's about the same question as the editor-in-chief of *Vogue* wondering which young designer of today shall be tomorrow's delight.

It's going to be quite a search for the possible drivers of this new world order. Which of the social-economic beacons are no longer valid *in the eyes of the populace,* and what lies around the corner to reach full bloom—pregnant, but still hidden—as the underbelly of society is of an entirely new reality?

We are certainly on the lookout for whoever cries, "Feel! Hark! See! We are all pregnant with each other! And in the next election, we give birth to a completely new vision."

Who is/are the rainmakers of change upon whose vision strategists will construct their plan for the future? A plan that takes into account the belly of society but that serves its own interests in the first place?

To change the world, you need no more than two people: a mastermind and a brilliant populist.

Trump!

Donald is the brilliant populist genius, but where is the Mastermind organization that backs him, uses him? We will soon come back to this.

With this conclusion in mind—there must be a plan somewhere, and it is not Donald's—and the fact that we see Donald Centerfold every single hour of the morning talking/tweeting to America and the world, it should become clear that, while he has no fixed plan, he has/is playing a critical role so far in the plan of whoever is backing him up.

"If he has no plan, he is definitely a critical part of a plan." So Trump is the brilliant populist face of those planning and ruling for a new world order.

Assuming this, you wonder the following:

> "Whose plan might that be?"
> "What does this 'plan' consist of?"

Back to the "plan"

What do we know about the plan?

We know that it's there. That there has to be one.

Or that at least there's one in the making.

We know that its inventors aren't brash about it.

We know it's big, because it announces no less than the new world order. So the change embedded in the plan must be *big*…!

Who could want a plan for change of such a magnitude that it requires the unconditional narrative persuasiveness of the president of the United States himself?

As Donald Trump, "the chosen one," plays a key role in the plan, and as he entertains fairly right-wing ideas, we probably have to think in this direction.

Probably, economic motives play a role as well. Big business after all is part and parcel of the American social and political fabric.

But isn't big business doing well anyway? Why would it need a new world order so badly? Wasn't it the intention of the top executives of the American economy to simply continue with the present social and economic model?

"All power to globalization."
All wealth to bankers and other financial suckers.

Long live the exploitation of society,
of you and me,
of the State,
of the rest of the world!
And of Nature!

Why, you might ask, did the powerful American financial-corporate system suddenly back Trump *after* the primaries? The ones who swore to globalization and shareholder value—and fuck-all-the-rest creation, they would have loved to continue "globalizing" for at least another few years.

The answer is that Trump wrung the most successful economic concept of the last decades solo and with his bare hands. Or rather with his bare tongue.

Not because he liked this so much but because he wanted so badly to become president. And he understood that was what the underbelly of American society wanted.

And as soon as he understood, he put his brilliant populist eloquence at the service of voicing the laments of those who couldn't talk but surely could vote. For him.

And this is how he became unavoidable, because the belly of society loved him. He understood what they wanted.

Bye-bye globalization!

They quickly understood too. Corporate and Financial America.

Perhaps they disliked Trump's personality, but they were up against most of his dominant narratives in which the street found itself so well reflected!

By running for the presidency and by soliciting the support of that part of the population with which Trump never had anything to do nor had ever wanted to, he wiped the entire economic world view off the table.

But corporate America probably asked itself the other question: "What would have been the long-term outlook for corporate America anyway if it had continued doing what it did?"

How long did corporate America think to continue profiting from globalization as a guideline and a guiding principle toward excessive profit in an ever-slower-growing world economy?

How did strategists of the American financial and industrial establishment (which in America has strong ties to politics) perceive their own future?

To answer that question, I must make a detour to the world of concrete business.

Here we go.

How to get rich? Sector leadership

If one wants to get very rich, there's a magic trick.

It's called "monopoly."

You have to use the word sparsely, because monopoly smells of realizing a more-than-average, excessive profit at the expense of consumers, and that's a no-no. To take advantage by way of a monopoly is not allowed, but everyone in business dreams about it.

Monopoly equals absolute leadership in the sector in which a company is active.

These days there are many "quasi-monopolies." Many in the beginning were based on a major innovation, but due to globalization, it's become far easier to be first in conquering the whole world. Microsoft in the old days, Google, Facebook, Booking, Airbnb…

Once the terrain has been covered, you have the advance, and, voilà, there you have your monopoly.

And the monopolist dictates prices. Lobbies the governments.

The real gold is earned by companies who, in their industrial or service sector, know no competitors or have already exhausted those. Due to the sensitivity of the matter, I prefer not to give examples.

If competition, however, is scattered over tens or hundreds of smaller players, you shall never really get rich—only well-to-do if you work hard enough.

What in business jargon is called "the overall structure of the competition in the sector" has a major influence in determining future gains.

In between these two extremes—on the one hand the monopoly and on the other a scattered field of many small competitors—there are many sectors where four or five bidders, the big guys, divide among themselves a larger half of the turnover in the whole sector.

This competition structure is called an oligopoly.

As a structure it is perhaps somewhat less interesting than a monopoly, but it can still yield hefty profits under two conditions: a strong-enough concentration is required in sufficiently few hands, *and* a there has to be leader! (Again!)

Indeed, you will soon understand that there is a major difference between the following two situations:

- Four competitors in the sector are about the same size. They all have between 10 percent and 15 percent of the market…and break each other's necks. Or try to do so at least.
- Of the four competitors in the market, one represents a market share of 30–40 percent, while the other three each represent about 10 percent in total volume.

In other words, in the second case, we clearly have (yet again) a leader. That leader's leadership is based mostly on clear competitive advantages, such as his favorable cost position or his fast-paced innovation.

It is the leader who is the first to announce markups in the sector.

The others follow suit. He organizes/coordinates mostly lobbying initiatives for the entire sector. **By taking care of the entire sector, the leader of an oligopoly takes care of himself in the best possible way**. And by accepting his leadership, the others take care of themselves as well.

But when a smaller player does not accommodate this leadership, the leader becomes grouchy and starts attacking the business positions with customers of the rebellious competitor and starts conquering market share by way of discounts.

His prices then become so attractive that the competitor who doesn't yield to his authority loses business… until he realizes that perhaps he's far better off for his own profitability by introducing a similar markup with his clients.

And so the job is done. The leader showed muscle, and the rebel acquiesced. Big balls, deep pockets.

The leader decides and guards over profitability for the entire sector. This is for himself the most profitable strategy.

This practice nearly comes close to what we call price agreements or "collusive market strategies," and those are incriminating punishable. Meanwhile, the customer loses in this type of "sector-wide collusive strategies."

Monopolists and leaders of oligopolies are sweet people as long as their decisions are followed and as long as they don't get the impression that their leadership is questioned.

But they can display extremely malignant behavior whenever someone is so bold. Poor, oh the poor man who dares to question their authority.

Power and authority are men's favorite toys. Once they have it, they never give it up.

And hell to whoever tries to snatch it away from them.

Challenging a leader

Once in a while, it so happens that the leader is challenged. Like Chronos, for instance, the god out of the Greek myths who ruled the world with his brothers, the Titans. He was killed by Zeus, who in turn acted in retaliation for the murder of his father Uranus.

Mostly, leadership contestations aren't so explosive, and in the business world, many of the provocations start slowly and unobtrusively.

At the outset, the leader—let's call him "Biggie"—doesn't even notice a very small new competitor called "Smallie," let alone perceive him as a threat. More often than not, they even do business with each other.

Smallie, however, is ambitious. He fares well, takes risks, and slowly gets bigger.

He's a fast learner and learns a lot too from his dealings with Biggie. Smallie, in the process, raises his market share but remains small in comparison to Biggie's dominance.

Smallie can become successful due to many factors and the many things he does really well: sometimes by offering better service and mostly by putting his products on the market at very competitive prices. If you want to gain market share, it helps to be smaller and faster. And he certainly is because of an organization that is young and far more agile, newer production methods, and possibly employees who are better motivated and want to work harder and longer than Biggie's.

Then the moment comes for Smallie to appear for the very first time in the minutes of the Board of Directors of Biggie. Because Smallie just sent out into the sector a "special offer" by which Biggie's clients can buy at very attractive prices by signing a "volume contract on call for one year."

As a result, Biggie sees his sales figures drop more than he likes.

This is a key moment in the life of an industry leader: Will he further allow Smallie to snatch from him market share, or will Biggie mobilize his leadership and teach Smallie a lesson?

This he does by dropping his own prices even below the level of Smallie's to make it very clear that the time for niceties is over.

And suddenly Biggie's Board of Directors starts seeing Smallie in a totally different light.

As a leader, Biggie cannot allow that too much market share be lost, and so he has to keep down his own prices to maintain the sales volume within budget.

- If he doesn't drop prices, he keeps his margins but loses sales volume at a deadly pace;
- If he lowers his prices only a little—a "watch out" signal to Smallie—this one doesn't take him seriously and continues with his commercial attack on Biggie's leadership;
- If his prices sink too deeply, his sales figures augment in volume, but he loses margin, and he cuts into his profits. And this makes the shareholders unhappy.

But so be it. There is no choice.

And the leader "flips."

Mentally, he is changing his whole way of looking at the market overnight.

A totally new market strategy with new rules becomes law.

For a long time, Biggie's strategy consisted of *accommodating* the small and ambitious Smallie. When Smallie became big and strong, Biggie **declared** *war* on Smallie.

The moment in which strategy "flips" isn't determined so much mathematically as by the "irritability" and risk profile of Biggie's CEO, his closest collaborators, and a handful of trusted people.

When is it time to flip?

When the leader says so.
When does the leader say so?
When the leader feels it is time.

Whether Smallie, after a price war in the market, succeeds in taking over leadership or whether Biggie successfully defends his is not important. You never know beforehand. More important is the financial losses during the transition period.

What is important is that inevitably a flipping point takes place in the heads of Biggie's management from an old to a new market equilibrium in a new market structure.

This goes along with a period of great instability and important conflicts in the market. This happens not only in economics but also in politics, in the animal kingdom, and in the playground in our kids' schools.

Let us stretch this analogy to geopolitics. The industry sector then becomes the world scene. The United States then becomes the leader Biggie, and the "flipping" by the leader sounds a lot like "the new world order" that Trump is talking about.

More than likely the megastrategists in the United States had started to show some concern about the future state of affairs—even in Davos the tongues had started wagging, by golly!—and so it became a matter of time to contemplate change.

But then came Trump.

And Donald Trump is clearly not an expert in oligopolistic strategy and tactics.

With the support of "the streets," Trump singlehandedly closed the door of the current political and economic world order behind him.

Time to flip!

Is there a plan somewhere on a hidden table from which it has to emerge that a few strategists in America have "flipped" about America's internal and international politics, **because Trump simply gave them no alternative**?

A "decision and determination to flip the future course of America and the world compared to the accommodation strategy in the Obama and Clinton era? Somewhere…?"

With the strategists of some group of influential Americans who wield sufficient power to help a president get elected and next put America on a collision course?

And who understood that Trump has touched the underbelly of American society and thus promptly put an end to the paradigm of globalization, which had been a cash cow for the rich for more than twenty years?

A plan, perhaps merely a slogan, which has nothing to do with the capriciousness and unpredictability of Donald Trump's declarations? But of which the unpredictability of Trump is the trigger and an essential part?

When after the primaries it became clear that Trump held the keys to the voting behavior of the majority(?) of Americans in a brilliant way, the major strategists of influential groups could no longer ignore him.

So there was flipping, all right—a little sooner than expected, but what must be done, must be done.

They understood perfectly well that the belly of America had made itself heard and that a silent majority had suddenly found its voice in Trumpian street preaching, and this would put an end to globalization.

Wealth creation for the very rich based on the paradigms of globalization and excessive shareholder value would still have had a few years of traction. But this economic era wouldn't have slowly have come to an end, as people had warned at the World Economic Forum in Davos.

The belly of America and Trump as their trumpeter said: "Enough is enough!"

Gee. Ouch. Bad boys, you exaggerated again!

Greed and greed again!

Yachts…the rich and their dicks.

Let's flip and "make America great again"

So far, my intuitive hypothesis has been that the confrontation between Biggie and Smallie will occur on the world economic stage.

But can we concoct a Smallie in a discipline other than economics, one that starts irritating America to such an extent that it starts to flip?

If there is indeed a different Smallie that bothers America, it must bother a very big, powerful, and influential part of the American population to be able to count on its support for creating a new world order in the near future.

Who could it be?

- A powerful American or a wider *religious* network that has the uneasy feeling that the Christian world is being threatened by Islam;

- An influential *white* Caucasian group that has the feeling that "their" America is being threatened by immigrants from Latin America and the Middle East or, if you want, by the "chocolatitos": the ones not-so-white of skin;
- And of course, the powerful *economic* lobby that is afraid it cannot sustain its world leadership position and wealth creation in the future as it has done for the last thirty years through globalization, excessive shareholder value creation, and abusive growth to which Trump as the *porte-parole* of the streets has called a *halt*!

So, we have three possible alternative Biggies behind Trump: a religious nucleus, a hardcore racist one, or an economic power block.

Mind you, these highly influential groups may overlap in thinking and membership.

- If Biggie is the hardcore Christian community and Tea Party, then Smallie is in their view the Islam world.
- If Biggie is the alt-right community, then the (too) liberal democrats and the Democratic Party represent Smallie.

- If Biggie is the American industrial and financial establishment, then China is Smallie.

One of these three possible Biggies is the *dominant* core behind the development of a new world order. The third one in the list did not initially support but quickly embraced the "streetegic" ideas of Trump.

Of them, who is in the process of fine-tuning this new world order plan?

My intuition—and I certainly may be wrong—says that the powerful industrial and financial establishment of the United States flipped its way of looking at the World when it realized that Trump's nationalistic gut-felt speeches had closed the door of globalization as a superprofit-making paradigm.

And by the way, some people in the almighty financial and industrial lobby group might most probably already have concluded that the fat was already off the globalization soup.

It was a matter of time.

The American economy on a world scale is still the greatest, but in relative terms, it is not so almightily great anymore.

Indeed, would Americans' current greatness have endured if the American economy kept operating in the future as it did in the recent decades of globalization?

No.

The United States and the world as a whole are living the end of an economic era that was dominated by two paradigms: shareholder value creation and globalization.

Both paradigms created a society that operated very far removed from its necessary social-economic equilibrium—that is, a society with a lot of freedom and personal entrepreneurship but also with sufficiently strong governments that will and can put limits to the endless greed and abuse by the very rich. And the "casino-entrepreneurs."

In fact, these same economic paradigms that Americans invented and so successfully implemented with huge wealth creation for the American rich as a result are not so much running out of steam, but they inherently contain the second-order effects that fiercely backlash and undermine the very same objective these paradigms intended to govern: "America the greatest and the wealthiest."

Paradigms, social or economic, always rise as sphinxes out of the ashes of their predecessors.

These ashes are at first hidden—done away with as negligible collateral damage—but soon spiraling negative second-order effects of the previous era become the raging fires of today's society.

Short-term greed is such a good blindfold against the enlightenment of longer-term strategic thinking.

The brilliant fool Trump had his eyes wide open and later found in the industrial and financial lobby his powerful backing.

It would quickly pretend to embrace Trump as a person.

Ambassadors of Goldman Sachs, ExxonMobil, the private equity lobby, and the like decided to "help" the new president achieve "their" goal: the goal of sustaining the wealth of the rich and of corporate America.

Reading the executive orders signed by President Trump in no way seems to contradict this hunch. They only favor the very rich and don't care about the poor and the colored.

So "China must be Smallie."

And Smallie is indeed coming.

Fast.

Global outsourcing

Profits go North;
Added value goes East;
Society goes South.

The nature of an economy does not develop in a linear way.

Its growth is driven by social and economic paradigms.

These paradigms are reservoirs of potential growth based on new ways of thinking.

They are not necessarily true but are so generally accepted they need no justification or explanation anymore.

They have become the *narratives* that dominate the thoughts and feelings of the masses.

Some narratives are right.

Some are lies.

Narratives always work.

In the seventies, the popular economic paradigm was about spreading a company's risk by diversifying its portfolio of activities. As the portfolio paradigm went into excesses, second-order effects materialized, and returns diminished.

A famous example was ITT Corporation. From 1960 to 1977, ITT acquired more than 350 companies and grew to a global corporation with $17 billion in sales.

When the diversification paradigm backlashed, "Shoemaker stick to your trade" became the new paradigm.

A lot of operating companies in the portfolios were divested by the holding companies, and again a lot of value was created.

Following its conglomerate years, ITT also began restructuring. A lot of divestitures were decided, and finally the holding was split into three independently listed parts to increase, oh yes, shareholder value.

The world was now mainly dominated by mono-activity companies. Only a few but highly trimmed portfolio companies like General Electric were left.

It was Jack Welch, its CEO, who successfully spread the idea that you had to be number one or two in your sector to make money. (Do we smell "leadership" here?) CEOs had to do this mercilessly and implement Milton Friedman's new paradigm that companies *only* existed to make their shareholders richer, **whatever that should take**.

The CEOs very much liked this idea, as these shareholders immediately decided to "align" the CEOs' interest with the shareholders' own interest.

That meant the CEOs (and to a small extent other high-ranking managers) would be—apart from the bankers—the *only other* beneficiaries of this paradigm shift.

They welcomed the idea of getting filthy rich themselves.

The CEO who had been "the estate's caretaker" was suddenly entitled to sit and eat at the table of "feudal lords" and get fat and happy as well. "The stewards became part of the gents' class."

Bank employees started to consider and call themselves bankers while they invested their bonuses in real estate.

People in trading rooms sold "handpicked" shares to innocent customers but put the proceeds of their own huge bonuses in much less risky trackers of the Dow or the S&P. They hoarded the big remuneration of the traditional merchant bankers but took no risk on their own money, as real bankers used to do.

Not much later, a whole new financial industry would arise of watchdog analysts, commentators, and young arrogant "know-it-alls."

For many of them, "creating shareholder value" would quickly become

Fuck the employees.
Fuck citizen-like behavior.
Fuck ethics.
Fuck governments.
Fuck taxes!
Fucking leave us, shareholders and bankers, fucking alone.
Fuck regulation.
Fuck nature.
The hell with any obstacle;
We have no fucking time to lose.

In their eyes the whole society had become dehumanized, "objectivized." No respect. Only disdain.

From the poor all the way up to the good middle class, all were just objects whose labor and pensions needed to be stolen.

They were called the consumer base: überdogs who were tricked by doubtful marketing practices, and based on stolen personal profiles, who consumed the products cranked out by the same tired workers in a globalized economy.

Inside their companies they were called "human resources," like financial resources or raw materials.

Resources that you purchase, process, and either ship as finished products to the market or kick them out in the street when age or burnout strikes.

Then, all of a sudden, society exists again and should fucking take care of them again.

Society as the lemon for the rich.

Society that assumes the cost of educating their employees.

Society that built the roads on which their trucks drive.

Society that paid the subsidies and the tax breaks they demanded.

Society that took care of the millions of employees that they had burned out.

In their view the government was/is there just to profit from as much as they possibly could, and politics must be lobbied to ensure that the regulators—who used to be the protectors of the interests of society at large—let the corporations do what they want and keep their nose and their legislation out of business affairs.

This became the almighty worldwide paradigm of "shareholder value creation" that gained absolute power from the late 1980s onward.

The globalization backlash

Starting in the 1990s, the twin brother of shareholder value creation, called "globalization," which had arisen in the middle of the eighteenth century, would accelerate supersonically, like a flash. It would hugely facilitate the growth of the corporations that needed new and bigger markets to fuel their growth.

For the *industrial* world, globalization meant two things:

- I can *sell more* and more easily in the rest of the world, as there are less trade barriers.
- Above all, I can *lower my manufacturing* or, more broadly, my total supply cost by *outsourcing internationally* to countries where wages are a fraction

of what is paid in Detroit, Michigan, or Kansas, Missouri, or Düsseldorf in Germany. (This is called delocalization.)

The outsourcing of American manufacturing grew exponentially and conquered in its early days Singapore, but quickly thereafter Hong Kong, Shenzhen, India, Taiwan, South Korea, Malaysia, Indonesia, Vietnam, and all of China.

Not to forget Mexico, the Czech Republic, Poland, Romania, Bulgaria, and so on.

And most probably the Moon in the future, provided the hourly wages are lower there.

To give an example, look at the number of companies per country in today's supply chain that Apple outsources the production of components for iPhones and computers to.

About 60 are based in the United States, another 350 in China, and some 170 in the rest of the Far East.

The massive outsourcing of the American industry was a boost to their short-term profits, which were the result of this massive Merry-Go-Round organized by American (and European) corporations, always looking for a cheaper place to produce.

But two big "Buts" occurred:

1. The evolution toward an optimal global supply chain led to a great loss of *added value* and thus employment in the US manufacturing centers *at home*.
2. To a great extent, globalization of the supply chain goes hand in hand with *delocalization*.

   - Far more than just the simple manufacturing got outsourced over time; it included also sophisticated software development, medical R&D, and the production of active ingredients that go into the products for pharmaceutical companies and the like.
   - To be an R&D and marketing company, while delocalizing all the shitty manufacturing and supply chain to subcontractors abroad, greatly improves the *profits* for the outsourcing company but at the same time diminishes the *added value* within the company or within its country of origin.

- The essential substance of a country's economy shifts gradually toward the receiving country!
- Profitwise delocalization is a wonderful thing, *provided* you keep innovating.
- Your technological or design advantage gives you in fact a temporary monopoly, which does generate the excellent returns of a leader.
- This explains why profits of American corporations can soar, while their added value and employment in their country diminishes.
- This explains why growth looks limited to 2 percent in the American economy. Yes, American corporations grow…on the stock exchange and outside the country.
- However, when your subcontractor starts to market his own range of products, *he* has the advantage over you if your innovation slows down or if his R and D accelerates thanks to learning from you.
- An example: Facebook was an innovator. Today Facebook's Chinese equivalent called WeChat is far bigger as a company. It has become the innovator, and Facebook is merely becoming a copier of WeChat's innovative functionality. Alibaba likewise.

Welcome to China's *Wirtschaftswunder*.

As the American government was "brainwashed" by the industrial-financial lobby, the lack of good oversight of the consequences, and missing legislation led to a complete explosion of corporate profits at the expense of society at large.

Derailed equilibrium.

The politicians were under the spell of money and looked the other way.

On Martha's Vineyard, no blacks, no Muslims, nor hardly any Chinese "in sight," unless they're drivers, cooks, and "Yes, sirs; no, sirs."

Half of Trump's success is due to the previous generation of politicians who were neglecting the losers of globalization. How they live, where they live. Their dire situation isn't the result of their own laziness or stupidity, but of the arrogant, disdainful policymaking in Washington, Westminster, Paris, Frankfurt, and so on, based on the globalization/shareholder value narrative that led to the galling second-order effects we observe today.

A fertile ground for Donald Trump, whose rise to president he owes to all these categories of people he does not know, does not like, does not respect. They are merely an audience for his narcissistic self. How cynical and funny.

Brexit, too, was born out of the disdain of the English political conservative class for the lower class in the country.

The prevailing paradigm of "the trickle-up economy" was a nicer, more polite—some might say, typically English hypocritical upper class—way of proclaiming unlimited shareholder value creation.

The Conservative Party always blamed the European Union and Brussels as an escape for their own lack of care for society as a whole.

The bankers in the City of London screamed that the "populace" didn't know what it was voting for.

It knew damn well!

The sitting Conservative politicians, who blamed Brussels when Britain got the flu or got constipated, are still there or have secured some well-paid job.

The City bankers will manage; they are modern, forward-looking, and sit in the biggest tax haven in the world (behind the State of Delaware but well ahead of so many more exotic places). After all, the ones who have always paid the bill in history will pay again. You. The lower middle class, the workers, and the poor. But at least the English may live in a more human society once Brexit has come into existence.

Educating Smallie

While corporations were optimizing their short-term profits, they were, at the same time, "educating" foreign workforces in skills these countries would probably never have acquired otherwise.

Chinese are among the best learners.

Furthermore, since the early 1980s, under the new liberal leadership of Deng Xiaoping, thousands of Chinese were sent abroad…to learn.

China, the Smallie in our story, is thus basically sitting on a tremendous manufacturing capacity and many other *capacities* that US corporations transferred to them in the name of excessive American shareholders' short-term profits. (Beat the expectations has become the favorite app of CEOs, and the bonus awards are big.)

Today, the transfer of first America's and Europe's manufacturing capabilities, followed by their engineering centers and finally research centers, has led to the rise of a formidable competitor in many different sectors—from basic steel to smartphones and other high-tech applications.

I would not be surprised if the West would simply not be able to produce certain high-tech products, like OLEDs for instance, any longer as they are all produced in Asia today.

Combine this with the typical Asian entrepreneurship and hardworking mentality to get "a better place" in life for the children, and you get the picture.

At home, economic foresight doesn't look too good for the longer term

Innovation in the United States reportedly is slowing down, except for digitization, which power of making people redundant is cutting even deeper and farther into the fabric of society than globalization.

Investment opportunities are slowing down.

Private equity is sitting on $1.5 trillion that do not find investment opportunities. With around seven thousand firms around, where will they find the deals that will give the returns they were used to and the bonuses they still want?

The huge wave of privatization in the whole world seems to have slowed down for the time being.

TTIP could have created an opportunity for growth.

With the private "investor–state dispute settlement courts," European countries would de facto give up their sovereignty.

What a superb victory for the financial world.

They can not only continue to get what they want by charming top politicians (such as Draghi, George Osborne, Barroso, and so on) but now, they would be able to bypass the country's legal system with the creation of the TTIP privatized courts of exception, who can fine governments if one or other corporation finds that a government is protecting its population too well against unchecked corporate greed and limits their social extortions.

Respect for the sovereignty of countries has always been the cornerstone of international law.

In the past, violators of the sovereignty principle were called traitors of their country and in the best of cases were decapitated without inflicting too much torture.

Today they are called TTIP negotiators.

If we want to limit the sovereignty of countries, let us start with countries like Sudan, Syria, and so on—not with European countries.

We don't need privatized courts where abusive corporations can come and force governments to abandon their basic societal obligations such as health care (the NHS in the UK, Krankenkassen in Germany), pension funds, railroads, social security funds, and the like.

A government is not a shop full of goodies, where corporations can come and shop (or steal) for growth.

Let everybody keep their fucking hands off what the basis was and is of the Western European Rhineland society model.

Continental Europeans do not need Anglo-Saxons to be taught sociology.

Robotization seems a very interesting area for innovation and growth. But again, American robots all seem to be produced in the East. It will create great manufacturing opportunities in the East, while making huge crowds of Americans redundant in their workplace.

No wonder, the new government puts so much emphasis on robot technology that "brings back added value" from the East and lets robots not replace, but work jointly together with American workers. This is the Co-Bot technology (collaborative robot) in which the United States is currently investing so much money.

Not only lower-skilled manufacturing and transportation jobs (driverless cars and taxis) but equally higher-paid jobs (banks) will be lost en masse. Take, for instance, the rise of robot advisers who replace former commercial bank employees to give investment advice.

The huge government project to redeploy all these redundant people is reportedly called project "Oblivion."

And what about the skyrocketing "social" digital economy? Are they superb entrepreneurs? No, they aren't "social" at all. They're just a bunch of illegals.

Uber, Airbnb, and others are deriving their competitive advantage from practicing illegal business. The so-called holes in the market that they found are merely based on ignoring all social infrastructure that has been put in place for decades to make this society indeed a "society" and not a "wild West."

They are the pirates of today's economy.

Facebook and Google are even worse.

Why can the law not force Zuckerberg to allow people to pay a monthly fee for their Facebook page say for $10 a month?

Why does the law let him exercise a full monopoly while stealing our lives and privacy against our consent?

Why can you become a Facebook member in two clicks, and why does it take a fucking two years to be forgotten by Facebook? Crooks.

Approaching fast the limits to economic growth:
excesses of unbridled "shareholder value" and
"globalization" lead to fast, abusive depletion of
Planet Earth

Apart from emptying the Western economy from its substance (added value, the income of the working class), there is another phenomenon that jeopardizes a future that looks like the past sixty years.

You surely have seen very many people walking the street who measure five feet seven (1.70 cm) or six feet. To see people who measure seven feet (2.13 cm), you must go and see an NBA match.

But have you ever crossed someone who measures eight feet?

Our global economy is like human height:

"it ain't coming without limits."

The shortening distance to the wall of depletion that will mark the end of unbridled growth is predictable and predicted already behind the closed doors of the board rooms of energy, food, water, and other companies.

It is the result of dividing the finite exploitation potential of the resources left on the planet by the pace of depletion by which our greed is abusing it, all the same ignoring the potentially disastrous (again) secondary effects.

Politicians who disagree should know that only silicium, salty water, sand, CO_2, and nitrogen are infinitely available on this planet. The rest have a limited supply.

There are just not enough earth resources left over time, and we are grabbing them too fast.

Our economy watchers placed their hopes on innovation and a thriving service economy in order to sustain unlimited growth, but it is hard to imagine that a world only consisting of bankers, lawyers, lobbyists, accountants, fiscal advisers, and consultants, who mutually sell each other services, is a sustainable model for the world economy.

Or countries whose industrial companies have become "R&D + Marketing" companies, whose managers have never seen employees actually "doing something old fashioned like building the damn product. Of which the entire supply chain is outsourced, which from my personal point of view seems unsustainable.

Surely, subcontracting as much as possible to lower-cost countries improves the margins and maximizes the return to the shareholders, but it also eats *the inner substance out of your economy.*

It resembles someone who has a thousand likes on Facebook but no longer real-life friends.

This economic model wouldn't work either, if it were chosen as a business model for a sub region in the world economy, or a "service-driven-only" business model.

Take Greater London.

Imagine what will be left of it after a real depression, let alone a war.

Where will the bankers buy their food supplies?

Pay with what? With advice? With junk bonds? Derivatives?

(The right answer is they will all be gone in time.
Flown away in their private jets.)

Service-driven economies are happy as long as there is abundance around, not when a downturn hits and hits hard…Oh my!

Business people who are able to look more long term sense the enormity and the end of today's abuse.

Energy strategists have known this for a long time.

Water strategists know this.

Sugar strategists know this.

Asian and Latin America soy planters know this.

And you may feel so too.

Taking stock

The world will change rapidly with the current groundswell induced by Trump, flipping from globalization toward a centric attitude toward own nation.

Maybe it also has some good consequences.

It may make politicians feel responsible again.

The ones who haven't heard or understood the rumbling sound of the belly of the "streets," like Theresa May in the

UK, will be laughed off with this highly effective English mixture of pity and disdain.

Instead of lazily "subcontracting" the well-being of their country to a bunch of greedy, short-sighted business entrepreneurs (TTIP), politicians now have to stick their necks out. Time for real statesmen and women to stand up and rise to the challenge of power in a democratic setting.

Make choices that big businesses won't like.

Take decisions that restore a sustainable equilibrium in society between the greed of the rich and the pain of the poor.

This is—if you are still capable of attributing something good to Donald Trump—his beneficial impact on politicians.

It is not difficult to agree that Donald Trump put a halt to globalization, but which idea will he introduce to the party in exchange for that?

Only the alternative of a war economy has the potential of creating a new economic surge for growth in the United States. *Tant Pis pour la populace.*

In a society where normal people don't count, this is the owners' best of all bad alternatives for economic policy.

The best policy undoubtedly is a globalized economy on the condition that it is kept in check by politicians and hasn't spun out of control to be a shameful social farce.

Actually, there is little to reproach big companies and ruthless entrepreneurs, except that they got far too much leeway for maneuvering us all into the dark space of money and nothingness.

The real blame lies with politicians of socialist parties in Europe and the collusive behavior of the Democrats in the United States with the world of money.

They are foremost to be blamed for our societies in shambles.

"Long live the stock exchange," though: the ultimate expression of a free market economy whose growth is carefully managed by our beloved central bankers…
Till the next likely crash.

Folk like President Donald Trump, his team, and his backers are risk takers.

They go for daring strategies for a maximum of profit that is possible despite possible losses when the world turns in reverse, and their decisions turn sour.

To unleash a war is no problem to them, unless a bomb would be dropped on their new private jet or on the putting green of their favorite golf club.

They pride themselves on introducing deal making and other management techniques into the governance of the United States of America.

Well, if you take too much risk in business and it turns out to be a big mistake or if you simply aren't lucky, you go bankrupt. And you start all over again.

President Trump is this principle in person.

Take too much risk with your country's future, however…
and…

Ethical and sound politicians display a totally different risk behavior than reckless entrepreneurs in business.

They go for a social loss that is manageable in case the world turns the wrong way. They put a limit, therefore, to the amount of downside risk that is taken, in case the whole community has to pay for it.

How irresponsible, for instance, is Mario Draghi, the Central European Bank leader. He is not managing the stability of the Euro. With a central bank balance sheet that is now approaching an astronomical 5.000 billion euro, all he has done is manage the upward trend of the stock exchanges.

The rich get richer.

What a good Goldman Sachs boy he is.

"*Vendu, vendu!*"

By doing so, there are no instruments anymore or ammunition to remediate the damage when the next financial crisis will (soon) break out.

In any given situation, two entirely different strategic options are possible. That is precisely the difference between governing a country and managing a company.

The statesman minimizes the greatest possible loss should the world be heading the wrong way. The other maximizes profits if the world heads the right way.
His way.
And when things go wrong…who cares…
"Après nous le déluge!"(Next time better.)

Do you want a reckless former air force fighter pilot to fly the jumbo that had to bring you safely to the other side of the world? Or do you want to put your daughter in an Uber car with a drunkard behind the wheel?
Or do you want…
Why then adore would-be politicians who are drunk on money and on themselves and who brag about the risk they dare to take?

The transition from a world that is no longer based on global leadership and coexistence, but on a conflicting contest for world leadership, is a huge and risky endeavor.

Don't leave this in the hands of Trump. (His clever friends know this too.)

In fact, Mike Pence would probably make a "great war president" in as far as this exists: he would be cold, calculated, and such a breath of fresh air compared to court jester Trump. At least…in the beginning.
Maybe that was the reason why he was silently, almost innocently, and consciously chosen.

Trump for the "putsch on power," Mike Pence for the "après-Trump."

Changing the world's blueprint, as is suggested here, based on the alternative world view of planetary confrontation, will bring on a formidable period of uncertainty, imbalance, etc.

Compared to this effort, the plan for the implementation of Brexit in the UK will look like a piece of cake.

And if the war with China needs to be, we must hope that American leaders are really thinking things through this time.

One wonders what kind of a war the next one will be.

Will it be fought on the Internet? Yes.
Will it be fought on the ground and in the air like before? Yes.
Will the latest integrated communication and artificial intelligence (AI) decision systems be used? Yes.

Will robots, drones, and underwater drones try to limit the number of body bags returning home from the battlefield? Yes.

Will nuclear missiles be deployed? I can't see the current generation of politicians having the nerves and the staying power not to use nuclear devices.

Three

PREPARE THE HEARTS AND MINDS OF
THE AMERICAN PEOPLE FOR WAR

From a strategic point of view, there are at least four major areas for the White House to be preparing the United States for a war of this scale.

Needless to say, you need an excellent military infrastructure with trained, disciplined men and women, and deployment of the latest technology on information, robots, and drones.

And the United States has that.

They also have a lot of recent battlefield experience due to their relentless quest for world peace abroad and for the preservation of human rights worldwide.

Here are four areas of preparation to get ready for a full-scale war:

1. *Prepare the hearts and minds of the American population at home (broad support base).*
2. *Rethink the planetary chess board of international alliances with other countries / organizations.*
3. *Repatriate supply chains, manufacturing, energy, and transport infrastructure (strategic independence in times of war).*
4. *Convert the business to a war economy.*

This book will not elaborate on the technicalities of making the United States internationally independent on its manufacturing and supply side, energy, and its conversion to a war economy (points 3 and 4).

Trump needs to repatriate jobs from China and Southeast Asia if he wants to engage in war with them.

You cannot fight the very same country that makes so many parts for the products and the equipment you need for that war and to get your whole economy going.

Building a broad base

What rough beast
Its hour come round at last
Slouches towards Bethlehem to be born?

—*W. B.YEATS*

Hundreds of years ago, French kings knew you couldn't start a war when two conditions weren't met:

As wars were expensive, you needed finances. Very fast. Plentiful. This is what banks were for, which most often were in the hands of Jewish bankers, who were deprived of the right to own land. They lent the king large sums of money, and citizens then paid dearly for many years to raised "war taxes."

Today, this type of financing is less of a problem when you are big enough and when you fare well in the bond market. You simply create debts that don't have to be repaid. They simply roll over through time. And still.

The most important matter though was garnering the support of the people, the citizens, the underbelly of society. Because they had to let their sons die "for God and country," have their horses and wheat confiscated, and with a smile on their face, and in chorus, sing the praises at mass happenings of the courage and valiance of their king.

In case you lacked the support of the populace and the lower rural nobility, the country rebelled, and the king had to forsake this war party with his foreign royal colleagues.

Oh my! How sad! What a pity.

In this respect the world hasn't changed a bit. Today, still the populace takes to the streets when it finds that "power" has gone too far.

- There were thirty-five million street protesters worldwide against the declaration of war by the United States against Iraq in 2003.
  But they were unlucky because Dick Cheney, Carl Rove, Donald Rumsfeld, and Tony Blair lied themselves through the propagandist fight and got what they wanted.
- Look at the street protests today in favor of Erdoğan in Turkey. He's at liberty and at ease to declare a war tomorrow.
- Millions of protesters for and against the election of President Trump…

Can Donald Trump announce and unleash war, against China for instance?

Well, he has always had *half* of the Americans on his hand, and they have stopped thinking.

These Trump fans only feel. They feel hope.

It is hoped that he will help them get out of the economic rut. (I was told by a Russian source that it is Donald's plan to reduce tax rates for all people without income to nearly zero.)

It is hoped that he will reintroduce "dying at the stake" for all gay couples and all desperate women who had an abortion.

It is the hope of white self-proclaimed superior people, of Trump fans who would rage against any folk, as long as they're not white, for instance

Blacks the N…s

Mexicans the…rapists

Arabs the (potential) terrorists

Asians the…gooks

Europeans…

It is the firm hope of people who know they have God on their side.

The discourse of a brilliant orator such as Trump is dominated by promises and manages to express the deepest, hitherto unspoken wishes of large parts of the masses. Trump can easily mobilize and prompt them—devoid of any reason, but united in a collective that is foisted upon them—to go along with his "subhuman" narratives.

Against any proclaimed enemy of one's dear old native land.

But that is only half of the population.

What about the other half? If Trump unleashed a conflict today, then a quasi–civil war in America, which would see two halves of the population diametrically opposed to each other, would be a more likely scenario than that the—what today is brandished by Trump as the elite—that is, the 51 percent who voted against him, normal citizens with an education and enough common and civil sense and compassion—would support him in that.

This second half of the American population——and thus a considerable part of the Western world——first has to be *psychologically massaged*.

Massaging the masses

Donald Trump's brilliant skill is exactly this.

Whether he is conscious of it or not.

You do not have to be a strategist to see this.

Trump, the supercharming, macho, reality TV superstar!

A seducer or a "media siren" is always needed to massage society.

Trump and his buddies behind the screens are the proud owners of a gigantic psycho-massage parlor:

it is called "the world."

On the menu of their "massaging services," the following items appear:

- First, beat the resistance of people to mush by totally *confusing* them.

- Meanwhile, incite/approve expression of public feelings of *vulgarity* among the populace and induce a general feverish resentful explosive mind-set in the country.
- Reprogram American DNA with dominant narratives—the famous *false truth*, also known in dictator countries as indoctrinating sheeplike behavior through propaganda.
- Focus the societal fever for an intended war (*Kriegsbegeisterung*) by trumpeting and repeating the name of the enemy.

Make the population crazy,
Let the testosterone call for hatred.
Once the enemy declared,
Let the drones fly,
Let the robots march
In the name of the Lord
And for peace on the entire planet.

Here comes Biggie!

Confusing the people first is key to their subordination

Every dictator must be jealous of Trump.

He gets more airtime for his personal propaganda than any dictator dares imposing in his own nationalized press and on TV.

And for free!

This book does not depart from the kind of a fascination for the person "Trump" that makes everyone want to know every day whether Donnie has eaten well and on whose head he has pissed again.

True, this hunger for sensation is the bread and butter of the media who helped to "make" Trump.

And truth be told, he does not keep them hungry.

Contradictory tweets are rapidly and frequently fired off.

For months, the liberals have been beside themselves.

Not only do they have to defend women, Mexican immigrants, Muslims, the LGTB community, natural resorts, the climate accord, the North Pole, and blacks against police violence, but half of America spoils them as "elitist." So they quickly resort to defending themselves.

To have to fight on so many fronts at the same time for the conservation of, or so they thought, established rights out of the old world order (remember?)—is it any coincidence?

Perhaps.

Or then again, no.

In chapter 1, we came to the working hypothesis that the White House, backed by the strategists of the powerful financial and industrial lobby, prepares for a war with China.

It then becomes thinkable to see in the randomness of accusations, vulgarity, and changing opinions of Donald Trump before and after his election a perfect tactic to break the opposition of well-meaning, mostly well-educated people.

These tactics were probably not really premeditated—it's just Trump the way he is. But when strategists saw him destroy the "globalization idea" in his indomitable way, suddenly it became very clear where the economy in the next years would *definitely not* be headed.

"Well, let's see it as an opportunity!" they must have thought.

His total unpredictability in the hands of a few good strategists might just as well help to get the American people where you want them to be, if your alternative for the broken globalization principle is a contest for worldwide leadership——namely, on its knees.

Trump bewitches people.

Many in this world wake up and go to bed with news about Trump. Today, already a little less than yesterday, and we come back to the necessarily temporary and transient character of his current fame.

His impact on people's thinking is altogether small.

But what he makes them *feel* is enormous.

The frequency with which Donald Trump scuffs half of American society and the world, day in, day out, deserves respect.

It's not everyone's call.

This is a series of occasional ego trips by a brilliantly narcissistic improvisation talent who randomly, liberally, and royally dispenses one-liners and smacks-in-the-face based on the latest inputs of his entourage.

Donald is a brilliant verbal processor; give him an audience, and he's happy. Maybe the people in the wings behind him are just calculating.

Were Trump's public presences conceived well before with this aim, they would have been part of a brilliant communication plan, staged and timed with the precision of a Swiss watch.

Each time one of his vulgar narratives—let's call a spade a spade; Trump, Trump; and dirt, dirt—let loose in the air by him, loses some steam, and liberal Americans have just about regained their senses…again, voilà! The next narrative is already being served to the media, and in no time it consumes the attention, the consternation, the wrath, and the adrenaline of Americans and the world.

So it seems his absolute priority to give Americans no time at all to debate something or to collectively draw conclusions that bind them as a people.

I don't know whether that's his purpose, but it is certainly his effect.

And they are getting oh-so tired.

The indefatigable Trump requires so much of their emotional energy.

He himself is playful.
But the others do take him seriously.

If their being tired and feeling that abrasive powerlessness keep doing their jobs, then people will stop organizing Sunday marches on Washington.

Instead, they will watch TV.
They'll watch Trump, dulled and tired of protesting.

There are only six large media companies left in the United States.

At least if one discards Facebook, Twitter, and Google as media companies, because Zuckerberg in Washington said they weren't one. Nah!

Is the oligopoly of the ten biggest media companies not even capable of the joint decision to organize a Trump-free day each week? To give us some time to get repose from the mad ride on the Trump tweet carousel?

Steamrolled by Trump's crushing unpredictability, the next conclusion about what is happening today with American society doesn't seem that far off the mark.

First they get angry, then numb, and then crazy.

What if this is precisely the (temporary and preparatory) role of Donald Trump in "the plan": get to power with the support of one half of the population and then stun the other half of the population.

Breaking their ideals for society, and because they nowhere find grip, drive them eventually crazy?

A role that suits him to a tee.

The dirty manipulation by social media

Isn't that interesting?

Social media aren't media.

That is the reason why traditional media as such are subject to legislation and regulation. But social media aren't.

So then why are dogs subject to legislation (they need vaccinations and cannot pee on the sidewalk, for instance)?

Answer: because dogs are social (Post-Truth, Trumpian logic)

To be social means you are exempt of legislation.

The legislation only applies to media who are not social.

But what about media who only have the word "social" in their name but who are, in essence, not social at all?

Social media aren't media, but Facebook, for instance, delivers more than 60 percent of all news via news feed to its American members.

Facebook, Google, no media companies? A bunch of crap.

A society only exists by virtue of a few truths and values shared by everyone.

When this commonality of thought disappears, society collapses too.

Because society is a living organism—think politics—there is a constant stream of dispute needed around any new situation or a political opinion or a new law, by which society verifies whether they suit its fundamental values and truths or not.

It is by *the confrontation of different viewpoints* about a certain issue or news item *among* the citizens *themselves* that a society can define its own synthesis and collective viewpoint about whether something is worthwhile or not.

Independent from its politicians.

A society searches and recognizes itself in the clash of opinions of its citizens.

Look around: when differing opinions no longer communicate with each other, violence, conflict, and extremism are never far behind.

The manipulation by social media of your news feed, which supposedly makes a selection via profiling of what most likely counts for you, is a flagrant deed of incivility.

A direct attack on the authenticity of our societies.

Precisely this preselection entails that we never again hear the ideas of people who think differently.

Where minorities in the early days were kept "behind bars," they are now being silenced behind the filters of perverse algorithms hatched by people whose only aim is personal gain, despite the fact that it leads to an incredible impoverishment of society.

Profile-dependent news feed creates numbness, because no one builds his opinion on a common fact base.

Companies such as Cambridge Analytica will further splinter cohesion in society in a deliberate way.

He who invented this carefully organized chaos created in fact a very smart, modern version of the *divide et impera*, one of the favorite tools of abusive power in the history of humankind.

Add a few million dollars' worth of astroturfing on top of the profiling/filtering/personal massaging approach of "social" media, and you've figured out the way the extreme right controls the pace of society's developing madness.

Therefore our "social media" society is breaking down.

Social media create isolation, fault lines, digital ghettos.

And in this fashion, our prejudices become "post-truth" truths, from which follow contentions, intolerance, and, at long last, extremism.

In the 1990s, the media became unbelievable powerhouses by the sector's endless concentration.

They were also no longer obliged to separate "facts" (remember that?) from today's op-ed pieces (opinions of politically motivated journalists or individual idiots who were carefully screened and briefed for completely biased street interviews "straight from life" for television news). This is undoubtedly one of the direct causes that American society has landed in the maddening quicksand of the Post-Truth era.

Fox News: "Everything is news and news is entertaining." Everything is plausible, but what is truly true?

A good definition from before the year 2000 of what a TV news journal used to be: "the most boring but trustworthy of all reality TV shows."

But soon, someone would rise and change the news on all channels (on TV, radio, newspaper, social media, and the most advanced of all Twitter) and turn it into the most vulgar of all real-time entertainment in the country and the world.

And where is the star? The blond, handsome, blue-eyed, wealthy, eloquent, seducing, supercharming, self-assured, spontaneous, creative, indulgent, crass playboy who will seduce the hearts and minds during prime TV news time?

Trump as a storyteller and king of vulgarity: a child of these times

Something that truly helps in preparing and massaging people for war, and of which Donald Trump makes great use, is vulgarity.

It is the perfect means to harden one's soul and soften one's conscience.

Trump is perfectly suited to lead a mass meeting.

To vulgarity.

"Yes, my dear nono-in-the-third-row-I-now-look-deeply-in-your-eyes-as-a-real-father. Please shout, 'Lock her up' as hard as you can."

And everybody shouts, "Lock her up! Lock her up!"

And Trump is standing on the podium.
Laughing. His body language approving.
Everybody can see it. This is allowed.
Education stinks.
Long live ignorance, vulgarity, and violence.

His personality has not a single problem with public counterviews, with rigging of facts, with slander by people, or with blatant misinterpretations of history.

Trump likes to lie, just because he dares. "Yes, I can!"

His lies sometimes border on ignorance. All the same, he seems to indulge in it when people are powerless, become angry, or are completely awestruck by his boyish, grotesque, and grandiose expressions.

Donald's vulgar expressions are basically the mature equivalent of a child throwing a temper tantrum in front of mummy. He's "acting out" against the world.

They are at the same time also Donnie's own psycho-controlling toolbox over the masses whom—contrary to what he says—he most probably doesn't like at all, let alone cares for.

He just likes the streets as an audience and as a gauge for his power.

And this is how you become president.

It may take years before respectability will come into fashion again with the American populace, as a "civil" principle in our dealings with each other.

In fact, this is a very creative way to realize one of his election promises.

"The swamp of Washington."

I thought he would make it disappear by mucking it out, but instead he is simply turning the whole nation into a swamp.

As a result, Washington looks clean now.

Hence, the swamp must be gone.

Trump did not teach his country to read and write. But he did teach it to shit and lie.

Being president takes a different bag of skills, however, than what it takes to become one.

Mike Pence, for instance, would make a great president…

We will come back to this.

By the way, would it be imaginable that the new president of France, Emmanuel Macron, actively incited the crowd and let it shout about Marine Le Pen, "En tôle! En tôle!" (Lock her up! Lock her up!) on his campaign tour?

Would he not—in Europe—himself be locked up, because of slander and incitation to violence?

Just imagine this summer that Martin Schultz, while campaigning in Germany to become chancellor, encourages the crowds to shout…

"Lock her up!"

Angela would most probably preserve her calm and conjure up from the deepest of her great heart and the fastest of her physicist's brain her magic "is-this-a-smile" smile.

Would we see on German television the crowds go as crazy as the Americans we saw time and time again last summer?

Wouldn't Martin Schultz not be locked up instead?

We must hope so.

One may start wondering about the dark side of American society.

Is its conservative, white, envious, deeply religious, Protestant soul having problems to accept the fast liberalization process of society over the last twenty-five years?

Time for revenge? Trump?

The dark angel preaching to the repressed American soul, to its underbelly—the white, honest, hardworking, religious, proud, and angry American people who are scared for the future, left behind by their (Democratic) leaders?

Trump is reprogramming the "social genes" of American society

- ~~Respect the law~~? Lock her up!
- ~~Be good~~? Be rich!
- ~~Help the poor~~? Fuck these idiots!
- ~~Be educated~~? Be vulgar!
- ~~Respect an artist, philosopher~~? They are useless losers!
- ~~Go to Mass~~? Go to Mass!
- ~~Love your neighbor~~? Hate your neighbor!
- ~~Behave~~? Do as I tell!
- ~~Arabs. Islamic. Terrorists~~? Whoever!
- ~~Act out your repressed emotions~~! It is fine.
- ~~Lie~~! It is fine.
- ~~Lock up a presidential candidate~~! It is fine.
- ~~Torturing~~! It is fine.
- ~~Break the law~~! (if you're very rich) It is fine.
- ~~Avoid taxes~~! It is fine.

On narratives

Dominant narratives are a terribly powerful social concept and easy to understand. Narratives are the verities that people remember when they have stopped thinking.

Every dictator understands intuitively what the power of narratives entails from the time he was still in primary school.

The narratives dominate the playground.

And whoever understands narratives will become master of the playground.

The power they contain is formidable.

A dominant narrative is the argument, the slogan, or the conviction that rules over the conversations between people in the street.

Has it already occurred to you that many people can learn a page of prose or a long poem by heart, but no one can remember a page full of telephone numbers?

The reason is both our great skill of storytelling, our joy to listen to them, and our great love for one-liners, punchy ideas that can "kill someone" and make bystanders burst out laughing with just a few words.

We love stories, and we adore storytellers.

The dominant narratives that ruled the social wisdom of the streets as a rule used to be carefully crafted by the upper class of intellectuals of a society.

Ideally, they struck a *balance* between greed of the very rich *and* a minimal care or respect for society at large.

In some periods of history, greed was sustainable (well, kind of).

The rich understood that the lower classes will only let them be sucked like a lemon as long as this populace can feed and educate its children, so give them at least the hope for the kind of better life they never could have had themselves.

So, a society dominated by rich people is *okay*.

Even for the poor.

The social narratives would control society.

Remember the shortest ever social narrative? It dates from the seventies in the United Kingdom.

TINA.

(There is no alternative (TINA) to breaking the back of the UK's traditional industry.)

But one shouldn't exaggerate.

What happens, however, when a society is dominated by rich people who suddenly consider themselves godlike, and above the law and who get away with tax avoidance, corruption, and worse…when they *show their disdain for those* middle-class people who can't even afford university for their kids anymore?

That society is doomed to be short lived.

Give a man the life of a dog, and it's fine.
Take away his honor, though, or the food for his children, and you will see what happens.
How the dog reacts.

It gets even worse when these rich are not old-fashioned entrepreneurs like Ford, Carnegie, Bill Gates, or Larry Ellison, but Goldman Sachs investment bankers, bond traders, derivative experts, private equity partners, hedge fund managers…all these "empty value" vultures who created and constitute this world together, which is summarized by such an expensive and polished yet such a vulgar word: "the financialization of the economy."

There is one interesting characteristic about the people in the streets.

It is their capacity to accept the lies of power if they are repeated frequently enough. They still will not believe them, but they will accept them and learn to live with them as a factoid of life. Narratives.

Humankind is the most flexible animal there is on the planet, and it can tolerate, endure, bear, and suffer a lot.

But social narratives are not eternal.

Remember what history tells when the citizens' scales fall off their eyes; when the belly of society starts to rumble, the beast gets out of the gutter and roars in awe of the super yachts.

Today, the vulgarity of Trump, his unpredictable behavior, and his favorite verbal narratives are becoming the dominant narratives for an ever-bigger part of an aggressive, nervous, touchy society.

Summary

Donald Trump did secure victory in the election.

He did that by surfacing and mobilizing the heaviness, the sadness, the anger, and the misery in the underbelly of the

American society: of those left behind by the tolerant, global world view.

But he did/does more to society: he is preparing the hearts and minds for indecency. And thus potentially for war.

Decent people do not go to war.

Unless attacked (not almost attacked nor a bit attacked nor afraid of going to eventually be attacked).

Only people whose mind-set is based on regressive and repressive emotions like fear, Power, or megalomania take the initiative for war.

He is playing that role brilliantly: prepare the American people for mass madness as a precondition for its leaders to engage in war with China.

And then?

You may wonder how his role may last in the coming years, and what else might he do in this superb political play that is called Once upon a Time in Reality *but to go home at (or before) the end. Donald Trump got the Republicans back into power. "A job well done, Donald! Thank you. We will manage it from here."*

Four

Rethink the International Chessboard of Strategic Alliances

Five hundred years of European history is basically all about a few royal families fighting with each other.

Their objective: European supremacy, a monopoly position of power, or preventing the other from doing so by preserving a balance of power.

France, England, Russia, and the Austrian Empire were the biggest contenders.

Germany did not exist at that time (it was only created in 1871). Instead, more or less the same territory as

Germany today was then called the Holy Roman Empire: it was more the reason *why* the others were fighting each other (to annex parts of the weak Holy Empire) than it was a contender for more power itself.

But at different moments in time, Poland, Spain, Sweden, parts of current Italy, and, not to forget, the Ottoman Empire (now Turkey) made attempts for European territorial annexation or dominance too.

Or at least they were afraid that other countries would make an attempt for dominance and tried prevent it.

But remember the example of the oligopolistic structure of the competition in certain industries, as described in chapter 1.

Likewise, not one single European country was strong enough and capable enough to rise to real European leadership.

It was the time of alliances.

And these alliances were very "flexible." They constantly changed over time. Everyone "slept" occasionally with everyone else, but the love affairs were short lived.

When the Austrians became too powerful, the Russians and the French got together to preserve the power equilibrium in Europe. The English and the "Germans" got together to beat French Napoleon in Waterloo.

At other times, the Russians and the Ottomans (the Turks) got together to rebel against the Austrian royal house Habsburg.

Europe was a poker game between royal houses, each with their ambitions, strengths, weaknesses, and predominantly the character of their sovereign.

Changing alliances (based on distrust) for centuries had been the *mot du jour*.

The fundamental reason for constant warfare in Europe and why this eternal quest for supremacy left the continent in a lot of misery but never with a clear winner was the fact that (again) there was no clear leader!

Indeed, a powerful and influential Germany as we know it today did not exist.

Existing instead at the heart of Western Europe was a very weak conglomerate, consisting of many principalities, called the Holy Roman Empire. It was a giant on feet of clay.

It was a collection of very powerful (purely feudal) regions in the center of Europe, owned and ruled by powerful princes who collaboratively elected their emperor.

The emperor was indeed the emperor, but his successors weren't chosen via bloodlines from father to son/daughter.

They were elected.

There were about twenty very important princes in the empire, who together chose the next emperor.

This is why these princes were very powerful and were able to evict the emperor when he asked for new taxes to pay for some war taking place on some other side of Europe.

"Me first!"

The Holy Roman Empire had a rather decentralized federal power structure, in actual fact.

Prior to the election of a new emperor, a lot of lobbying went on by the surrounding countries—the French, the English, the Russians, the Italians, and others—at the time. All the neighboring countries around the "precursor" of what is now located in the center of Europe and called Germany wanted to ensure that the new "boss" of this Holy Roman Empire would be on their side.

They tried to influence the election results by secretly "buying or influencing the votes of the twenty princes who together formed the "Emperor Election Committee."

They promised future favors to them, very much like what happened in the voting process for a new FIFA boss today.

So, what the Soviet Union did to the American elections or what the United States via the CIA does to influence the outcome of elections in other countries—for instance in Latin America—is not at all new; it is as old as Europe is.

(Lobbying is one of the more despicable practices not invented by Washington, but at the royal courts of Europe.)

Does this governance structure from a distant European past remind us of something contemporary?

For instance, the present governance model of the EU? *Copie conforme* or perfect copy of the government structure of the old days in Central Europe?

Democratic for sure, but weak in times of change. Bismarck changed things back then.

We had to wait until 1871—only 150 years ago, one hundred years after the creation of the United States of America in 1776 and around the same time as the American Civil War, which led to the United States as we currently know it—for Bismarck to come around. He was the prime minister of Prussia.

He seized an opportunity to unify the princely structure and strengthen the power in the center after the French were beaten by them.

He created the modern, centrally led country called Germany.

The European leader was born.

But the supreme game of alliances was not over. Germany felt encircled and squeezed by "unfriendly" countries, who in turn got scared by the power and expansionist ambition of the German emperor. When Germany heavily increased its military budget, it was perceived as a nascent threat.

Was there a "Biggie" in the making? Yes.

Again, alliances were made in the beginning of the last century; the French, the English, and the Russians got together to "get ready." The same alliance was formed in the Second World War, and, had it not been for Churchill and the involvement of the United States, Germany would probably have extended its formal leadership over the entire European continent.

For those readers who like to look at the world in a static way, just a reminder that the Western world as we know it today in Europe and the United States is not even two hundred years old.

The power chessboard of Europe—then—looks very much like the planetary chessboard today.

There are only three countries today that have sufficient strength *and* a sufficiently large zone of influence to be called real world powers: the clear leader of the West. They are the United States, Germany as the leading country of the EU, and "Rising Smallie" China.

But there is a whole slew of countries that cannot be ignored in the world power game, as they may be powerful allies leaning toward one side or another.

Under the leadership of the United States, this oligopoly with Russia, the EU with Germany (UK, France, Italy…) as primus inter pares, Japan, India, Brazil, Canada, and a few smaller ones functioned well.

The leadership was clear: the United States.

The rules were set: peace and global trade without obstacles.

Damn Smallie!

Damn China!

And damn Trump, who does not understand oligopolistic sector strategy.

However, as soon as the United States as the leader changes its world view, all current international alliances in the world are up for grabs, a lot like what happened in Europe in the past.

Every (group of) country(countries) is diplomatically sleeping with many others. The diplomatic merry-go-round is spinning round and round. And the key questions remain the same, as always:

Who can best help me defend my current position?
Who can best help me achieve my ambitions?
Who can best help neutralize the ambitions of others?

Under the hypothesis in this book that the final objective of President Trump is to confirm, sustain, and fight for

US military and economic supremacy over the planet, all traditional alliances need to be investigated and checked whether they are still relevant for the United States to achieve *this* goal or not.

And the answer is *no* or *maybe*.
Maybe to NAFTA.
No to TPP.
No to NATO.
No to the Climate Change Paris Agreement.
No, no, no to…

This new situation seems to create nervousness and confusion among political leaders.

The tweets in this area destabilize the current alliances.
It is surprising to understand why they do.

Is it not crystal clear that the United States wants to shape its best team and have for the remainder its hands free when it prepares for hostility?

The world should be thankful to Trump for his early-morning tweets. They prepare the heart and minds of the actual allies for action.

They kick many complacent politicians in the ass.

How kind of Trump.

Every tweet on international policy is a *lettre d'adieu* for a broken friendship since time immemorial.

On Russia

"Two-front wars" are always more difficult to win for a country that is squeezed in the middle. There are many examples in history.

Opening a second front by your ally requires the common enemy to split its military resources and weakens its military thrust in combat on both fronts.

Logistics become a nightmare.

If you were the United States, and you were preparing for a war with China, then Russia would become a natural ally. All the more so, since Russia has always considered China as a far more real threat for its country than the United States.

Russia would force China to an important deployment of military resources in the north and west of China, while the United States could concentrate their enormous military power on the front with China in the southeast, the Pacific, and the South China Sea.

Moreover, China would no longer be able to count on the raw materials, oil, and gas coming from Russia.

(In fact, China and Russia together would make a formidable combination for raw materials, technology, land, and people. Fortunately maybe, they are not the best friends.)

A blockade by the American navy, which would be tacitly accepted/supported by the Philippines and Indonesia, would upset the strategic supply of China greatly.

Would this not be a very plausible explanation for the recent rapprochement of the United States to their classical enemy, Russia?

(Forget the recent "I like you; I hate you; I help you; I punish you" as played for the press.)

But such a landslide in planetary power balance remains a very delicate exercise—something that normally is being "scouted" via ultra-secret diplomacy.

This is similar to the equally important alliance talks in the playground of an elementary school. If a young boy in the playground of first grade wants to invite the girl of his dreams to have an ice-cream together but isn't quite sure whether she will say yes, what does he do? He sends over his best friend to ask in his stead if she'd be interested…

In European diplomacy, business was conducted in the same fashion. Here, it was more likely a count or a duke who was very close to the king or who likely was part of the king's own family. He went abroad incognito to measure the water temperature on the other side.

Hence, it seems evident that "exploratory contacts took place" between Trump's campaign team and the Russian power structure.

Trump couldn't publicly declare that he was close to a "deal" with Putin, if he weren't almost sure that Putin wouldn't finish him off in the media afterward.

Hence, it makes a lot of sense that Trump's most trusted adviser or family member had contacts early on with the Russians to take the temperature for such an alliance.

If it were you, and you were to move to a new world view that requires new alliances to *"Putin* place" wouldn't you do the same?

But to cooperate to this new world order, Putin also wants something. He must have asked what's in it for him.

He wants to regain control over Eastern-European states, which he regretfully saw depart westward after the fall of the USSR, depart in the direction of the West, worse still with certain former Soviet Union countries even getting NATO membership.

Isn't this the unifying mission of Vladimir Putin? To want back the Eastern-European territory that was lost after the fall of the Soviet Union in 1991?

This is the reason why the brilliant strategist and tactician Putin had every interest in the victory of Donald Trump.

In case Hillary Clinton had become president, she would have maintained the present world order with regard to China and Russia; Russia would have continued under economic sanctions; and she would have maintained a strong NATO, which under American military curatorship in Europe would have made the Russian expansionism toward the West entirely impossible.

Are the approaches and all the secret contacts between Trump's campaign team before the election and his "trusted advisers" a prelude to that?

Has Putin therefore "lent a hand" to get Trump elected and to soon ride the wave of his new "world view" in which suddenly there is *again room* for Russia on the stage of the world's very great?

An alternative explanation for the reconciliation between Trump and Russia would be the dependency relation of Donald Trump himself in relation to Russia. It is suggested that Trump's business is dependent upon Russian financing.

It is hard to believe that this hypothesis has never been denied so far. This is just a matter of reading his company balance sheets, and Americans are usually pretty good at that.

A third alternative explanation would be a sensual affair between Donald—*l'homme à femmes*—and a Russian beauty while he was staying in Saint Petersburg.

Within the context of this book, the most likely interpretation for the contradictory signals Trump gives about the future Russian–American relations would be a total change of strategic direction by the Americans vis-à-vis Russia—and hence Europe, and hence NATO.

In any case, Putin's position is very comfortable as he sits and watches the leadership game unfold between the

United States and China. Waiting patiently for offers as both could benefit from an alliance with this powerful man and this key country.

Consequences for NATO

What then is NATO's future?

One day Trumps *says* he remains a big defender of NATO, the other day NATO is no longer necessary, and later again NATO is just about tolerated, but European countries are required to contribute more financially.

This gives Europe a headache.

But to what conclusion is the anti-China strategy of the United States leading?

If Putin offers help to the United States in its endeavor to choke China's ambition for world leadership, then the United States has to give Russia a free ride into Europe to "repossess" some of the countries that were part of the old Soviet Union, which fell apart in the early nineties. This is the quid pro quo.

Otherwise Putin doesn't play ball.

But this type of deal making is impossible if the United States is also *on the other side* as the defender of a free Europe through its leadership role in NATO.

NATO has to yield to enable the American, anti-Chinese alliance with Russia.

Consequences for TURKEY

Another brilliant strategist is Turkey's president, Recep **Tayyip** Erdoğan. That Turkey would have liked to become a member of the EU became very clear early on.

The rise to power of the religious-minded Erdoğan makes for a more and more outspoken Islamic character of Turkey. Erdoğan turned his back on the liberal heritage of Turkish founder Atatürk and the liberals who for decades had run the country.

Besides, Erdoğan understood perfectly well what lived in the underbelly of a large part of the Turkish people: a return to the sure value of religion.

In the history of Europe, conflicts often took place on one of its two flanks—in the western part or on its eastern borders.

An alliance between the Russians and the Turks (the former Ottoman Empire) as was the case in the past against the Habsburg and/or the Holy Roman Empire—the precursor to Germany—would not really be a first in European history.

And the world may comfort itself by saying these two countries and their leaders hate each other.

Nobody, however, dares to affirm that international alliances are as stable as the borders of the countries that unite them.

And hey, are those two not President Trump's "new" buddies?

What a blow to NATO if Turkey were to leave. What a wide-open weakness on Europe's southeast flank, and what a border to protect all from Finland's north of the Arctic Circle, all the way to the south of the Greek islands and the border with Syria.

Consequences for Paris agreements on climate change

Armored vehicles, fighter jets, and most battleships do not operate on solar power. Nor on wind energy.

Not only is the concentration of maximum power obtained by solar cells to drive these fantastic engines not sufficient, but solar power does not work too well in a war zone.

Imagine the driver of an armored vehicle who radios to his battlefield commander that he cannot move for the moment because he first has to clean the mud from his solar cells on the top of his vehicle.

Or, "Let's stop the fight until tomorrow morning, guys; the sun is going down."

Like in the European Middle Ages.

Many of the fighting devices (even new high-tech drones and robots) are (not surprisingly) made of metal.

And iron foundries and steel mills do not operate on a grand scale of solar energy.

Aluminum smelters need insane amounts of energy, and I want to see the solar cell park that will supply them of all the energy they need.

Finally, in times of war, the supply of goods and energy has to follow the war front. Solar cell parks don't travel well.

In short, war is a fossil-fuel-based business.

Would this be the reason why President Trump is favoring fracking?

Favoring new drilling close to natural reserves?

Turning federal land over to the states that can "turn them over to business"?

Is this reportedly to fuel the economic growth, or is it to become strategically independent for the required type of energy and raw materials in times of war?

War is a very dirty business, and it is perfectly understandable that President Trump does not sign a "clean contract" with the rest of the world while preparing "a dirty all-polluting war."

One has to choose in politics: one decides to go either for a cleaner world or for war. It is one or the other.

His withdrawal from the Paris agreement is, I am sure, a pure matter of personal decency. I guess.

Uncertain consequences for other countries

My knowledge of geopolitics is too limited to elaborate on how the merry-go-round of affinities, common interests, I-scratch-your-back-if-you-scratch-mine negotiations may unfold in the next five years and could make some of the important countries lean toward one side or the other—China or the United States.

We can be more-more-than-less sure about the position of Israel. But what about India for instance? How will the match India–Pakistan play out? And the match between Saudi Arabia and Iran?

An interesting case is Mexico—one of Trump's darling victims during his campaign and early on in his presidency to spit on.

How can one see the American society operate without the Hispanics?

This is like the British National Health Service (NHS) operating without any nurses coming from the European continent.

Did the Mexicans really kick white Americans out of their jobs, or were they instead welcome in America to do the jobs many Americans—men and women—didn't want to do anymore themselves?

Trump will need a lot more workers in tomorrow's war economy. Winning a war is not only a matter of technology and army quality. It is also a matter of demographics.

At the end of the Second World War, the Americans produced as many fighter planes in one week as the Germans could in one month. Guess who won.

The wall between the United States and Mexico will never be built.

As mentioned earlier, a good mutual economic interest between countries may actually turn out to be a stronger motive for making an alliance than ideological reasons or the emotions that some politicians have the mouth full of.

On diplomacy

On a more conceptual Pre-Truth note—it is a well-known fact that the degree of difficulty for people to communicate in a group or a project team increases exponentially with the number of people who are involved.

At least when there is no clear leader.

Now imagine the diplomacy, the second-guessing, and the paranoia smoldering underneath the surface among the members of the G7 or the G20 (or G40), who each individually try to optimize their position in a nervous, unstable world where the United States has given up its leadership role.

Gone are the days when Henry Kissinger said, "At four o'clock in the morning, they all speak like me."

The huge diplomatic effort to come 'round on a world scale can probably best be compared with the infighting among Arab leaders that happens in the Middle East today. (Another interesting case to follow of a leadership contest—regional this time—is between Iran and Saudi Arabia)

One has to be able not only to name the countries and find them on the map but also understand the character and the ambition of each of their landlords, warlords, and politicians; one has to understand their relations with each other, understand what happened between them in the past, and get an inkling of where these relationships are heading in the future.

This mastery sounds more like a Netanyahu than a real Trump skill! His nonchalance is the last thing that immensely complex and careful secret-alliance diplomacy needs to be successful.

And all this topped with today's nervousness of people and their leaders who do not know history and who want their wishes for wealth and growth to come true here and now and ASAP and immediately!

To me it feels like playing chess on a chessboard with hyper-active chess pieces that have been electrified, equipped with roller skates, and suffer from ADD.

All this during an earthquake.
Guess who wins?

And Europe?

Ai, ai, dear old Europe! Time to move the retirement age, get fit again, come to grips with your reality, and solve your problems.

Under the assumption of this book's main idea, a huge challenge remains with Europe. How to join its forces against this formidable Russian enemy, who until now was only kept in check by the enormous military presence of American troops and intelligence services in Europe?

How to become stronger and independent?

Not only in military terms but also on the information front!

If Europeans communicate over the Internet with each other, they do so through Google, Facebook, Microsoft, Yahoo, Twitter…

All American controlled.

If they buy something somewhere, they pay with Visa, MasterCard, American Express, Citi, PayPal…

American controlled.

Location apps on smartphones are mostly of American origin.

He who controls the highways and the hubs—be they physical railroads, harbors, and highways as before, or the information highways and satellite systems as today—will be in control.

The hardest task though is to change the European community's governance structure.

The century-old governance structure of the Holy Roman Empire—a weak emperor in the center, much power in strong, rich regions—makes us think of the current governance structure of the EU with an equally weak central structure in Brussels, and all weighty decisions are totally dependent on the ratification of all countries that are part of it.

Europe will have to get stronger.

Fortunately, we already got rid of the hypocrite Brits for whom a contract or a promises lasts as long as it benefits them and not a single day more.

If you want to win a soccer game, better to play with ten guys you trust than with an eleventh guy who makes an own-goal from time to time to block the team from winning.

Shall the leader who will truly unite Europe on a political and legislative level, and forge it into a power that can stand up to a new world order and to Russia, be born out of necessity?

By virtue of an outsider's breath? Putin? Trump?

Who shall be the dearly needed "Bismarck for Europe"? From which of the twenty-seven member states shall he rise?

Or shall it be a she?

Epilogue

The world is for sure a powder keg, but who lights the fuse?

It may or may not be Trump, but for sure the world does not need a strong jamming station like him when it is moving to a new world and considering big changes in geopolitical alliances.

We must hope that *international* politics will not be the reason why he will be remembered.

On the *domestic* front, it is hard to find any of his political decisions (or failed initiatives) that aimed at improving the life conditions of so many economically deprived Americans who voted him into the presidency.

There are a lot of executive orders to the benefit of his kindred, the very rich, and the big corporations.

These might be justified to make America great again.

They also happen to be very effective in the preparation of war.

Trump should not be remembered for that either.

Donald Trump will be remembered.
For his disruption.
And his transitoriness.

For the worse.

For single-handedly and abruptly disrupting global economic policy as a means to get himself elected.

For degrading the American state to the level of a badly managed company.

For managing the White House as the Executive Committee of an outgrown family business where all the members are smarter than their CEO and paterfamilias.

For turning delicate diplomacy into deal making with the mikes on.

For keeping the whole world under his spell while forgetting to be funny.

What else to say about him?

You can call upon the noblest of feelings to mobilize the people for war, for example, against fascism or against pedophile. This is easy and good.

However, with the Chinese it is different.

They didn't do anything except for working hard.

To mobilize the American people for this war, their dirtiest feelings (dressed up in their noblest disguise) need to be called upon.

Hate, fear, jealousy, envy, and the feeling that the strangers who threaten your supremacy are in fact "lower humans" than you are and hence not *entitled* to a nicer destiny at your expense. (Similar to how Arabs are wrongly depicted by some media.)

Creating a mind-set for a vulgar war is what Donald Trump did.

Replacing good behavior and education by vulgarity, racism, and aggression.

If the coming war is not a war of classes like the Spring of Nations were in Europe (the rebellions of 1848 and 1989), it will be a war for *planetary leadership.*

People may believe today that Trump's war will be against North Korea.

Or against ISIS and Islam. That the Middle East is much more than a training ground for perfecting new weaponry systems, combat experience, and territorial proximity to the oil fields of Middle East.

Still, ISIS and terrorism are very likely Trump's lightning rod. Get people warmed up. Nothing more.

Besides, in the contest for regional leadership between Iran and Saudi Arabia, the Arabs will weaken themselves internally.

Once again.

And after all, Israel is keeping an eye on the situation.

American politics keeps the narratives based on fear and disdain afresh in the hearts of the people.

The whole country permanently on red alert.

Terrorism! ISIS! Immigration!

But where are the American victims of terrorism over the last ten years if you do not count the American soldiers who died in Afghanistan and Iraq? Terrorism is very much a European problem and doesn't justify a permanent surveillance of all voice and e-mail messages of the population at large.

Let the specialized agents of the secret services do their jobs and the media stop sanctifying the terrorists and marketing more terrorism.

Donald Trump is not after the Arabs.

In his and his friends' eyes, Arabs are just a cumbersome side issue and an ideal group to be victimized, to line the American population up around a "vulgarity and lies" testosterone culture that breeds so easily followership.

So, let the Arabs not worry too much.

About Trump.

They should keep worrying about Netanyahu though.

It is the Chinese the Americans will be after longer term.

And then, in a few years, when the real enemy China is announced by the country's leader, the hearts and dirtied minds of the population will be ready to receive the new brief for war and will fight them with all their bottled-up hate and their ignorance—deeply convinced of the indoctrinated narratives of fear and supremacy, repeated and repeated all over again.

In the future, President Trump will be remembered like so many other top politicians.

"He did a lot of harm but did nothing wrong."

We should not lock him up

Smart, energetic, and inventive as he was as a boy, he probably was the pride of his parents, who—in their adulation—forgot to teach him limits and compassion for the less gifted and the world at large.

I am sure Donald Trump is a loving father and a good husband.

Trump has remained in the first place a mischievous boy. That is a gift of life that he should not waste on complicated and cumbersome politics.

Is he a bad president? He is brilliantly bad!

What is next for Donald Trump who excels in the skill that is required to become president? Not to be one?

No impeachment, no locking up. Please.

The Republicans in Washington should know better. Grateful for his giving the White House to them (or at least to part of them), they should spare him and all of us this disappointment.

Besides, the real problem is not President Trump but his powerful friends "behind the curtains."

The bright guys who surround him. Who found in him a superb *maître de cérémonie,* a charismatic reality-TV star who catapulted them all along with himself into power by a brilliant election campaign.

His role may soon be over.

These friends have big, cool, narcissistic egos.

They are the finest, most charming men, prospering in the world of money and life.

Mike Pence would be a fine replacement for President Trump.

And a good war president.

Unlike Trump, who grabs foreign leaders by their hand, he'd certainly grab them by their balls.

The world was never waiting for you to come, dear Mr. President.

For the Mothers

When Father Power embraces Mother Democracy,
Then fucks her with the help of the politicians of a parlia-
mentary system,
Strangles her and empties his poison
of austerity,
of taxes for the middle class,
Complete control over humans,
They're the first category of the "Internet of things,"
Repression of the people in the streets,
While favoring the very rich, and
Privileging legislation for their future,

WILL YOU THEN BE PROUD, MY SON,
To be a soldier?

WHEN YOU WILL SEE YOUR MOTHER WIPE
Her tears
When you depart for war,
As she knows
Father Power will not let you come back
As you are now.

No need to come back in a body bag.
Even when all your limbs are still hanging in the right place,
How screwed up will you be
In your head, your heart
When the ugliness of what you saw in war
Will make you forget forever your past
Longing for a beautiful life in the future.

www.ingramcontent.com/pod-product-compliance
Lightning Source LLC
Chambersburg PA
CBHW070807240726
48654CB00007B/250